Cultivating Healthy Habits

A Guide to Mental Wellness and Lifestyle Changes

Table of Contents

Chapter 1. Introduction

Welcome to a transformative journey of self-discovery! Our Special Report, "Cultivating Healthy Habits: A Guide to Mental Wellness and Lifestyle Changes," unlocks the secrets of living your best life. With a focus not just on physical health but mental nurturing as well, this guide takes you through practical and easy-to-follow steps towards lasting health and wellbeing. Based on proven techniques and backed by extensive research, the findings in this report promise to enlighten, inspire, and most importantly, empower you to take control of your health. Whether you're seeking a lifestyle overhaul or just want to add some wellness sparkle, this report is a compendium of invaluable tips, expert advice, and revolutionary insights. So why wait? Embrace the chance for change today! Dive into the transformative world of nourishing habits and give yourself the gift of lifelong wellness. Your journey to a healthier, happier you starts here.

Chapter 2. Understanding the Basics of Health and Wellness

Before diving head-first into the mechanics of health and wellness and how it affects each of us, it's crucial that we all understand what these terms truly mean and imply. Health, as defined by the World Health Organization, is a state of complete physical, mental, and social well-being, and not merely the absence of disease or infirmity. Wellness, on the other hand, adds an additional layer. It is an active process of becoming aware of and making choices towards a more successful existence.

Chapter 3. The Importance of Physical Health

Physical health, one of the three components of health, refers to the state of your physical body and how well it's operating. Our bodies are complex, dynamic systems that respond to daily habits and behaviors. Everything we do - from what we eat and drink to our level of physical activity and the amount of sleep we get - has a profound impact on our physical health.

Eating a balanced diet is fundamental to maintaining physical health. A proper diet can help regulate body weight, prevent chronic diseases such as heart disease and cancer, boost energy levels, and enhance overall life expectancy. Physical activity, on the other hand, benefits cardiovascular and muscular health, improves mental health and cognitive function, and can increase our lifespan.

On a larger scale, physicians measure certain health indicators such as blood pressure, cholesterol level, body mass index (BMI), and waist circumference, among others, to gauge an individual's physical health. By keeping these indicators within recommended ranges, we significantly reduce our risk of developing serious chronic diseases.

Chapter 4. The Importance of Mental Health

Mental health is equally crucial, and it is intertwined with our physical health in many ways. It includes our emotional, psychological, and social well-being. It affects how we think, feel, and act, but it also helps determine how we handle stress, relate to others, and make choices.

Just as there are habits we can adopt to promote physical health, there are strategies to boost mental health as well. Practicing gratitude, making social connections, getting enough sleep, eating nutrient-rich foods, and participating in regular physical activity can all contribute to better mental health.

Resilience, the ability to bounce back from adverse events, is a significant contributor to mental health. We can build resilience by maintaining positive relationships, accepting that change is a part of life, setting realistic goals, and taking decisive actions to tackle issues head-on.

Chapter 5. Social Health and Its Role in Holistic Wellness

Social health is another facet that contributes significantly to overall health and wellness. It refers to our ability to interact with people around us, to form meaningful relationships, and to influence social and community situations positively.

There's mounting evidence that social environments affect health outcomes, with social isolation and loneliness linked to higher risks for a range of physical and mental conditions, including heart disease, depression, cognitive decline, and even death. However, having strong social relationships might encourage healthy behaviors, such as regular exercise, a balanced diet, and adequate sleep, resulting in better overall health.

Chapter 6. Understanding Wellness: A More Holistic View

Although health typically focuses on physical and mental wellbeing, the concept of wellness encompasses much more. Wellness is often divided into multiple dimensions, including environmental, intellectual, occupational, emotional, spiritual, physical, and social wellness.

Each dimension of wellness can affect overall quality of life. Therefore, it is essential not just to focus on a single area but instead strive for wellness in every area of life. For instance, occupational wellness refers to satisfaction and enrichment derived from one's work, while intellectual wellness reflects a commitment to lifelong learning. Environmental wellness insinuates living a lifestyle that respects our surroundings, and spiritual wellness reflects a search for meaning and purpose in human existence.

Chapter 7. The Impact of Habits on Health and Wellness

Our daily habits have a significant impact on our health and wellness. Simple lifestyle changes such as adopting a plant-based diet, increasing water intake, reducing alcohol consumption, or adding a 30-minute walk to your daily routine can have profound effects on both physical and mental health. Being mindful of our daily activities and their impacts, and making necessary adjustments, can pave the way to better health and wellness.

In essence, understanding the basics of health and wellness requires acknowledging the interconnected nature of all these facets: physical, mental, and social health, as well as the many dimensions of wellness. A holistic view of health and wellness considers all these factors rather than focusing on any one element in isolation. After all, health and wellness don't merely mean an absence of illness but reflecting a complete state of overall well-being.

Chapter 8. The Mind-Body Connection

The human body represents an intricate network of interconnected systems, each operating symbiotically to achieve wellbeing. A significant part of this network is the profound connection between our minds and bodies, with research increasingly suggesting that our mental state can influence our physical health, and vice versa. To fully appreciate this intricate link, let's delve into the multifaceted aspects of the mind-body connection.

8.1. Understanding the Mind-Body Connection

The idea of a connection between the mind and body isn't new. Ancient healing practices, such as Ayurveda and Traditional Chinese Medicine, have espoused this link for centuries, focusing on achieving wellness by balancing the mind, body, and spirit. However, it's only recently that modern science is beginning to understand and validate this concept.

In essence, the mind-body connection refers to how our mental, emotional, and social factors can affect our physical wellbeing. It underscores how stressors, whether physical or emotional, can impact both our mental and physical health. Conversely, a sensation like pain can impact our mental wellbeing, highlighting the interconnectedness of our physical and emotional states.

Several scientific studies indicate that our thoughts and emotions can measurably affect our bodies. For instance, chronic stress has been linked to numerous health problems, including heart disease, digestive problems, and sleep disturbances. On the other hand, positive emotions such as happiness and optimism can boost our immune system, promote health, and extend life expectancy.

8.2. How Does the Mind-Body Connection Work?

Now that we understand the existence of this connection, you may be wondering how the mind communicates with the body, and vice versa. The nervous system, which includes the brain, spinal cord, and nerves, is the primary communication pathway. It's a complex network that sends and receives billions of signals between the brain and every part of the body, allowing them to communicate.

Hormones also play a crucial role. When we experience stress, our bodies release a "stress hormone" called cortisol. High levels of cortisol can eventually lead to health issues like heart disease, high blood pressure, and diabetes. Meanwhile, positive feelings can trigger the release of dopamine and serotonin, hormones that are linked with feelings of happiness and well-being.

Let's not forget about the role of our immune system. Accumulating evidence suggests that the mind can even influence our immune responses, further highlighting the intricate link between the mind and body.

8.3. Techniques to Leverage the Mind-Body Connection

Harnessing the power of the mind-body connection can lead to tremendous benefits for your overall health and wellbeing. Here are several techniques you can employ:

Mindfulness: Mindfulness involves focusing your attention on the present moment. Practicing mindfulness can help reduce stress, anxiety, depression, and improve physical health. Techniques can include anything from traditional meditation and breath work to mindful eating and walking.

Cognitive Behavioral Therapy (CBT): CBT is a type of psychotherapy that can help you understand the thoughts and feelings that influence behaviors. By identifying negative thought patterns, you can learn to control emotions, cope with stress, and manage physical symptoms.

Yoga and Tai Chi: These gentle exercises combine movement, meditation, and rhythmic breathing to reduce stress and enhance wellbeing. By focusing on the connection between your mind and body, yoga and tai chi can improve sleep, reduce pain, and increase strength and balance.

Positive Thinking and Self-Talk: Optimists live longer and healthier lives — this is a proven fact. Positive thinking isn't about ignoring reality or setbacks. Instead, it's about approaching hardship with a productive and positive outlook. Similarly, positive self-talk can improve mental and physical wellbeing.

8.4. The Power of the Placebo Effect

One of the most compelling pieces of evidence for the mind-body connection is the placebo effect. A placebo is a harmless, inactive treatment — like a sugar pill — given to a participant in a clinical trial, typically as a control measure. The surprising thing is, sometimes people who receive a placebo see improvements in their condition simply because they believe they are receiving a treatment.

This phenomenon demonstrates how powerful our beliefs and expectations can be in terms of their effects on our body.

8.5. Closing Thoughts

The understanding and recognition of the mind-body connection promise a holistic approach to health and wellbeing, offering an array of beneficial techniques that go beyond traditional treatment paradigms. By integrating physical care with emotional and mental health support, we have the power to use the mind-body connection to its fullest potential, paving the path for a healthier, harmonious life.

Indeed, without disregarding the importance of proper medical treatment for physical illness, mental care can play an equally important role in our lifelong journey toward overall health and wellness. Embracing this interconnectedness can help us create a well-rounded approach to wellness, one that lets us tap into our natural healing abilities, creating an environment of true reconciliation between mind and body.

Chapter 9. The Art of Mindful Living

Mindfulness, a simple yet profound concept, can drastically improve one's life. It is an art that requires patience and practice to master, but it offers significant benefits. It has the power to anchor us in the present moment, deepen our understanding of ourselves and our reactions, develop greater resilience, and foster inner peace.

9.1. The Principle of Mindfulness

Mindfulness is the result of harnessing the power of the brain to focus on the present moment, appreciating it without judgment. By practicing mindfulness, we can separate ourselves from our thoughts and emotions, allowing us to gain perspective and react calmly and effectively to any situation.

It's based on the premise that life unfolds in the present. Yet, so often, we let the present slip away, preoccupied with the past or anticipating the future. We become mindless — not in the present moment, reliving the past, and obsessing about the future.

Mindfulness helps us remain anchored in the present moment, enabling us to form deeper connections with ourselves and the world around us. Likewise, mindfulness is neither a panacea nor a magical remedy. It's a tool, a practice of turning into oneself and the world, of cultivating the capacity to control our focus and directions of our thoughts instead of being led by them.

9.2. Benefits of Mindful Living

A consistent mindfulness practice can bring about profound changes in your mental and emotional state, thereby improving your physical health and overall quality of life. These benefits fall broadly into five categories: stress reduction, enhanced awareness, improved mental health, increased compassion, and enhanced personal growth.

To begin with, mindfulness helps us manage day-to-day stress by teaching us to respond to stressors in a non-reactive and composed manner. Since stress-related illnesses are so rampant today, this has significant implications for physical health too.

Secondly, mindfulness increases our self-awareness. It allows us to recognize our habitual emotional and behavioral patterns and interrupts these patterns before they spiral out of control. Mindfulness practice enables us to respond more skillfully to life's challenges.

Thirdly, mindfulness can help boost mental health. Regular practice has been linked to decreased levels of depression, anxiety, and irritability. It can also improve sleep quality and concentration, and promote an overall sense of wellbeing.

The fourth benefit is compassion, both for oneself and others. Mindfulness cultivates a kind attentiveness that allows compassion to emerge. Also, by realizing interconnectedness between all beings, we naturally become more compassionate and empathetic.

Finally, mindfulness nourishes personal growth. It enables us to witness our thought and emotional patterns, which can lead to insights about oneself and promote changes that align with our deepest values.

9.3. Cultivating Mindfulness: Techniques and Exercises

Developing mindfulness involves regular practice. It's not about perfection but about recognition and returning. Here are some helpful exercises and techniques to cultivate mindfulness.

Mindful breathing is the simplest and most powerful exercise for practicing mindfulness. It involves focusing your attention solely on your breath, observing each inhalation and exhalation. When your mind wanders, as it will, recognize it and kindly bring your focus back to your breath.

Body scan meditation is another technique. This involves paying attention to different parts of your body, from your toes to the top of your head, and observing any sensations, emotions, or thoughts associated with each part.

A daily mindfulness meditation can greatly enhance your practice. Set aside a specific time each day to sit in silence and simply be. Focus on your breath and accept any thoughts and feelings that arise without judgment.

Mindful eating is another opportunity for practicing mindfulness. While eating, focus your attention on the foods - their taste, texture, aroma. Appreciating every aspect of the meal, and most importantly, chew your food slowly and thoroughly.

Lastly, there's walking meditation. This involves focusing on the physical sensations of walking – the ground beneath your feet, the swing of your hips. It can be a powerful way to connect with your body and the world around you.

9.4. The Power of Now: Living in the Present Moment

Mindful living isn't just about meditation and exercises; it's about incorporating mindfulness into your everyday life. Being wholly present and engaged in whatever you're doing significantly enhances the quality of the moment.

To start practicing, take a few moments every day to simply be. Whether you're doing dishes or walking to work, be wholly present with the experience. Fully immerse in the sensations – the cool water on your skin, the wind tousling your hair. Noticing and appreciating the small moments not only adds richness to your life but can lead to deep shifts in your world view.

To level up, you can designate specific mindfulness triggers throughout your day – everyday activities that will remind you to come back to the present moment. A few examples could be before eating a meal, entering a room, or turning on your computer.

Living in the present doesn't mean ignoring your past or not planning for the future. It simply means living fully in the present while it's happening. Remember, the present moment is the only one you're sure of. Living in it maximizes your life's potential.

9.5. Conclusion

Learning to live mindfully is a journey, an ongoing process. It takes patience, courage, and most importantly, practice. But every effort brings rewards that can transform your life. So, begin today. Take a deep breath, open your awareness, focus on the now. Your journey to mindful living starts with the present moment. Enjoy every step of this beautiful journey.

Chapter 10. Cultivating Healthy Eating Habits

The path to holistic health begins with food. Each nutrient that enters your system plays a vital role in maintaining and promoting physical, emotional, and mental wellness. Crafting a diet that addresses all these areas is a fundamental stepping-stone in the journey towards holistic well-being.

10.1. Understanding the Importance of Balanced Eating

Balanced eating is not about strict dietary limitations or depriving yourself of your favorite foods. It's about feeling good, increasing your energy, and improving your outlook for the long-term. Your diet can directly affect your physical health and impact your mental and emotional well-being.

A balanced diet involves ingesting a variety of foods that provide the nutrients your body needs. These nutrients, which include proteins, carbohydrates, fat, water, vitamins, and minerals, work together to promote good health and sustain bodily functions.

Chapter 11. Nutritional Components in Your Diet

Understanding the role of each component in your diet is crucial for cultivating healthy eating habits.

11.1. Proteins

Proteins are responsible for the structure and function of all cells in your body. They contribute to repairing tissues, creating antibodies that strengthen the immune system, and forming new muscles and blood cells.

Sources of high-quality proteins include lean meats, seafood, eggs, dairy products, legumes, nuts, and seeds.

11.2. Carbohydrates

Carbohydrates are the body's primary source of energy. They fuel crucial organs such as the brain and heart and keep us alert and active. Thoroughly understanding carbohydrates benefits us in disengaging from harmful dieting myths.

Opt for complex carbohydrates found in whole grains, fruits, vegetables, and legumes. They are rich in fiber and help control appetite and weight, reduce risk for heart disease, and maintain blood sugar levels.

11.3. Fats

Fats often carry a negative connotation due to their association with weight gain and heart disease. However, not all fats are unhealthy. Understanding the difference and including healthy fats in your diet can greatly contribute to wellness.

Monounsaturated fats and polyunsaturated fats, found in avocados, nuts, olive oil, and fish, are examples of "good" fats. They help lower bad cholesterol levels and reduce the risk of heart disease and stroke.

11.4. Vitamins and Minerals

These micronutrients perform various supportive roles in our body. For instance, vitamin A promotes good vision, vitamin C is involved in tissue repair, and calcium strengthens our bones. A varied and balanced diet can provide you with all the essential vitamins and minerals needed to maintain good health.

11.5. Water

Water plays a fundamental role in maintaining the balance of bodily fluids, regulating body temperature, and aiding digestion. Make sure to keep yourself adequately hydrated.

Chapter 12. Establishing Healthy Eating Patterns

Setting up a consistent eating pattern helps your body anticipate when your next meal might be, improving metabolism and digestion. Eating breakfast, lunch, and dinner around the same time each day can promote a healthier diet.

12.1. Being Mindful of Portion Sizes

Overeating, a common issue in our society, often occurs because we're distracted or eating too quickly. Grow accustomed to understanding portion sizes and practicing portion control to prevent overeating.

12.2. Eating a Variety of Foods

No single food can provide all the nutrients your body needs. Therefore, incorporating a variety of foods from different food groups offers a larger range of necessary nutrients.

12.3. Consuming Less Processed Foods

Processed foods usually contain high amounts of sodium, unhealthy fats, and sugars that can be detrimental to our health. Stick with fresh, whole foods whenever possible.

12.4. Enjoying Your Meals

Eating should not be perceived solely as a necessity, but as an enjoyable activity as well. Sit down for meals without distractions, chew slowly, and savor the flavor of each bite.

Chapter 13. Recommendations for a Healthy Plate

To visualize what your meals should look like, imagine a plate divided into sections. Half of your plate should consist of fruits and vegetables. One quarter should be protein, and the remaining quarter should be filled with whole grains.

Chapter 14. Closing Thoughts

Cultivating healthy eating habits is about making consistent, gradual changes towards a well-rounded diet. Every food choice you make is a chance to propel you towards your health goals. The objective is not to be perfect, but to feel energetic, decrease health risks, and be in good spirits as much as possible.

Remember, everyone's journey is different; what works well for someone might not work for you. Listen to your body, respect what it needs, and don't compare yourself to others. You have the power to make the right decisions for your health and well-being. So, will you make that choice today, for a healthier tomorrow?

Chapter 15. The Essentials of Physical Fitness

The journey to impactful physical fitness is multifaceted and diverse—it goes beyond just pounding the pavement or hitting the gym. To help you in this journey, we will discuss several essential elements that contribute to physical fitness, including regular physical activity, strength and resistance training, flexibility, and a balanced and nutritious diet.

15.1. Regular Physical Activity

Regular physical activity is the cornerstone of physical fitness. This is slightly different from exercise, as it involves all movement that increases energy use and engages your muscles, such as walking to the grocery store, gardening, or even house chores like dusting and vacuuming.

The World Health Organization (WHO) recommends adults engage in at least 150 minutes of moderate-intensity aerobic physical activity or 75 minutes of vigorous-intensity activity each week. You can even combine the two. This suggested quantity increases beneficial health outcomes and decreases risks of noncommunicable diseases.

15.2. Strength and Resistance Training

Strength training, sometimes referred to as resistance training, is another key to achieving physical fitness. This form of exercise often includes weightlifting or resistance band exercises and primarily builds muscle strength and endurance.

It's recommended you do strength-training activities at least twice a week. Aim to include 8-10 exercises that target all the major muscle groups in the body: chest, shoulders, arms, back, abdomen, hips, and legs. This ensures a balanced routine, preventing uneven development of muscle and reducing the risk of injury.

15.3. Flexibility

Flexibility is often the most overlooked aspect of physical fitness, but it's critical to overall health and exercise performance. This element is not about becoming the next yoga superstar but rather ensuring that your joints and muscles can move through their full range of motion. A regular flexibility routine can improve fitness performance, help prevent injury, and allow better movement in daily life.

Do flexibility exercises at least twice or three times a week. Most of these exercises can fit naturally into your workout regime or be done separately. Yoga, Tai Chi, Pilates, passive stretching, and dynamic stretching are great ways to improve flexibility.

15.4. Balanced Diet

Our bodies need fuel to function, especially when we're pushing them to their limits with physical fitness activities. That fuel comes from the foods we eat, making a balanced diet equally important as exercise in a fitness regimen.

Working towards a balanced diet doesn't mean you need to revolutionize everything you eat overnight. Instead, aim to consume a variety of nutrient-dense foods across and within all the food groups while avoiding excessive calorie intake. Make sure to include fruits, vegetables, lean proteins, whole grains, and healthy fats in your diet.

15.5. Rest and Recovery

Physical fitness isn't all about constant movement. Our bodies need time to heal and recover, especially after strenuous workouts. Rest days are crucial in any fitness regimen for muscle healing, rebuilding, and growth.

Aim for at least one to two rest days per week but listen to your body. Some people may need more rest, especially when first starting a new exercise routine or after particularly grueling workouts.

15.6. Regular Check-Ups

Regular health check-ups can ensure that your body is in condition to handle the physical fitness routine you're following. These check-ups can help identify any potential risks or issues before they become severe, keeping you safe and healthy on your fitness journey.

15.7. Conclusion

Achieving physical fitness is not an overnight task, but consistently following the guidelines discussed above can significantly benefit your health and wellbeing. Remember, the crucial part is to listen to your body, adjust based on your needs, and above all, enjoy the journey! Regular physical activity, combined with strength training, flexibility exercises, nourishing diet, ample rest, and regular health check-ups, is your path to physical fitness and the first step on your journey to overall wellness.

Chapter 16. Moving Beyond Stress: Techniques for Resilience

Stress - it's a condition we all deal with, some more than others. No matter the level, it's important to understand the impact of stress on our overall well-being. Be it long working hours, managing a household, or coping with personal grief, stress finds its way into our lives. The key is not to eliminate it, but to build resilience against it. Developing a lifestyle that emphasizes mental wellness can help us brave the storm of stress and come out on the other side feeling stronger and healthier.

16.1. Building Understanding: What is Stress And Resilience?

Stress is a part of life. It's a normal reaction to challenging or dangerous situations. But when it becomes chronic or overwhelming, it can severely impact your mental and physical health.

Resilience, however, is the ability to cope with adversity. It's about bouncing back from difficult experiences and not letting stress overcome you. While some people may naturally be more resilient than others, it's important to remember that resilience can be learned and developed.

16.2. Recognizing Stress: Signs And Symptoms

Stress manifests in various ways and can affect every part of your body. Some common symptoms include constant worrying, restlessness, lack of concentration, fatigue, irritability, sleep disturbances, and physical symptoms like headaches and stomach problems.

Recognizing the signs of stress is the first step towards practicing resilience. Being aware of your mental and physical state will help you make necessary changes.

16.3. Proactive Measures for Stress Management

Now that we've identified what stress looks like, it's essential to explore techniques to manage it. A proactive approach can include a combination of mental strategies, physical exercises, and dietary changes.

Mental techniques include mindful practices like meditation, relaxation exercises, keeping a gratitude journal, and cognitive behavioral techniques.

Physical exercise can act as a stress-reliever by boosting the production of your brain's feel-good neurotransmitters, known as endorphins. Committing to a routine that includes any type of physical activity can contribute substantially to reducing stress and building resilience.

A balanced diet is also crucial in managing stress. Consuming whole foods, maintaining a regular eating schedule, and minimizing caffeine and alcohol can significantly influence your overall stress levels.

16.4. Unique Techniques For Building Resilience

Resilient individuals manage stress more effectively because of their ability to adapt to adversity. Here are some proven techniques to build resilience:

1. Self-care: Prioritize your well-being. It's important to maintain a healthy lifestyle, including adequate sleep, balanced nutrition, physical exercise, and regular check-ups.

2. Setting realistic goals: Outline achievable steps toward your aspirations. These goals may be personal or professional. Meeting smaller goals can provide a sense of control and purpose.

3. Building connections: Foster strong, positive relationships with family and loved ones. Social connections can provide emotional support during times of crisis.

4. Developing emotional intelligence: Understanding and managing your emotions can help you react to stress more effectively.

5. Positivity: Try to maintain a hopeful outlook, allowing you to see potential solutions to your problems rather than focusing solely on the negative aspects.

6. Embracing change: View change as a part of life and expect occasional roadblocks. It's about developing flexibility in your thoughts, actions, and reactions.

7. Seeking professional help: When necessary, seeking assistance from mental health professionals is not a sign of weakness but a proactive approach to wellness.

16.5. The Role of Mindfulness in Building Resilience

Mindfulness, or the practice of being present in the moment, is a fundamental technique for stress management and resilience. Mindfulness can take many forms, from meditation and breathing exercises to mindful eating and walking.

When you're present in your actions and thoughts, stress and anxiety can lessen, providing a sense of calm and clarity. This awareness also allows you to react to stress in healthier ways, increasing your resilience.

16.6. Cultivating a Growth Mindset for Resilience

Developing a growth mindset, or the belief that abilities and intelligence can be developed through hard work and dedication, is a powerful tool for resilience. This mindset nurtures a passion for learning and a resilience that sees failures not as evidence of unintelligence but as a springboard for growth and stretching one's existing abilities.

In a stressful situation, instead of feeling defeated or overwhelmed, a person with a growth mindset will take it as a learning opportunity, an occasion to grow, to develop, and to move forward.

16.7. Conclusion: Moving Beyond Stress

Building resilience demands effort, patience, and practice. However, the potential benefits are worth it - an improved mental and physical health, a better quality of life, and an overall sense of wellness. The practices and techniques shared in this chapter are tools you can use to navigate life's adversities, manage stress effectively, and truly empower yourself to control your health and well-being. Time to make stress a stepping stone, not an obstacle. Your journey towards a more resilient you starts now!

Chapter 17. Sleep: The Forgotten Pillar of Health

Sleep, often dubbed the third pillar of health, serves as the restorative force that underlines the rhythms of life. While proper nutrition and regular exercise are consistently emphasized, the importance of good quality sleep is frequently overlooked in our busy modern lives.

17.1. Understanding the Importance of Sleep

The importance of sleep for health cannot be overstated. Scientists and medical professionals continually discover new links between sleep and holistic health. Chronic sleep deprivation has been associated with a myriad of health problems, such as obesity, heart disease, diabetes, and even certain types of cancer. What's more alarming is the toll of poor sleep on mental health. The correlation between sleep disorders, depression, anxiety, and lack of focus is now well established.

17.2. Vital Functions of Sleep

Far from being a passive state, sleep is a highly active physiological process where vital functions take place, including the restoration of energy, growth and repair of tissues and immunity, and cognitive processes like memory consolidation. In fact, sleep has been recognized as a state equivalent to nutrition: both are crucial for disease prevention and health maintenance.

17.3. The Connection Between Sleep and Mental Wellness

One cannot overemphasize the link between sleep and mental health. Lack of sleep impairs your cognitive process. It affects concentration, memory, mood, and decision-making capacity. Long-term sleep deficiency could lead to serious mental health issues such as depression, anxiety disorders, and chronic stress.

17.4. The Science of Sleep - Understanding Sleep Cycles

To effectively improve sleep habits, it is essential to understand the biology behind sleep. Sleep is divided into two primary types: rapid eye movement (REM) sleep and non-rapid eye movement (NREM) sleep, with four stages cycling through the night. During REM sleep, dreams occur, and the brain is almost as active as during wakefulness. NREM sleep is the restorative sleep when physical repair and recovery occur.

17.5. Sleep Hygiene: Transforming Your Sleep Environment

Sleep hygiene defines habits and behaviors in your control that can directly impact your sleep quality. The environment where you sleep plays a significant role. Ensure your bedroom is dark, quiet, and comfortably cool. Maintain a clean sleeping area free of random noises and distractions. Investing in a good quality mattress and pillow can enhance your sleep experience significantly.

17.6. Developing a Sleep Routine

Consistency is key in cultivating healthy sleep habits. Sticking to a specific sleep and wake time can help regulate your biological clock and optimize your sleep quality. Design a restful pre-sleep routine with activities like reading, yoga, or meditation. Avoid screens and heavy meals close to bedtime.

17.7. Nutrition: Its Role in Sleep Quality

What you eat can directly affect your sleep. Consuming high-sugar food and caffeinated beverages can disrupt sleep, while certain nutrients like magnesium, calcium, and B vitamins can improve sleep quality. Planning your meals and snacks consciously, and eating a few hours before bedtime, can aid in better sleep.

17.8. Sleep and Exercise: A Reciprocal Relationship

Physical activity can help regulate your sleep rhythms. Regular exercise promotes the duration and quality of sleep by boosting the production of serotonin in the brain and reducing levels of stress hormones. However, being mindful of your workout timings is essential to prevent potential sleep disruption.

17.9. Managing Stress for Better Sleep

Chronic stress or worry can lead to sleep disturbances. Practices like mindfulness, meditation, deep breathing exercises, and progressive muscle relaxation are beneficial stress-reduction techniques. You can explore mindfulness-based therapy for insomnia (MBTI) or cognitive behavior therapy for insomnia (CBTI) as well.

17.10. When to Seek Professional Help

It's crucial to know when self-improvement measures aren't enough and professional help is required. Sleep disorders such as insomnia, obstructive sleep apnea, restless leg syndrome, or chronic nightmares are serious health concerns that necessitate medical intervention.

Throughout this chapter, the mission has been to shed light on the importance of Sleep, the constantly overlooked, yet vital pillar of health. Implementing the advice provided will not only contribute to holistic health but also enhance overall life quality. Always remember, a well-rested body has a happier soul, making sleep not a passive necessity, but an enjoyable act of self-love and self-care.

Chapter 18. Breaking Free from Negative Habits

Negative habits can affect all aspects of your life, bringing about detrimental changes in your mental and emotional wellbeing, your relationships, productivity, and overall quality of life. Breaking free from these habits may not be an easy journey, but it's undeniably one of the most rewarding experiences you can undertake.

18.1. Understanding Habits and Their Impact

Before addressing the problem of negative habits, it's important to understand what habits actually are. Habits are patterns of behavior that have become automatic after repeated practice. When a habit is formed, your brain has developed a neuropathway that allows it to perform this behavior with less conscious thought and energy. This neurological efficiency is a double-edged sword: while it allows us to seamlessly perform beneficial actions like brushing our teeth, it also locks in damaging behaviors as habits.

Negative habits can cause a range of problems in your life. Physical symptoms are the most visible, such as in the case of unhealthy eating habits leading to obesity or illness. However, the mental and emotional effects can also be dire, often causing stress, anxiety, and depression. Yet despite the negative outcomes, many people find it difficult to break their harmful habits because of the temporary relief they often provide.

18.2. The Psychology of Habits & Habit Loops

Your habits operate in a three-part cycle known as the "habit loop." This loop is composed of a cue, a routine, and a reward. The 'cue' triggers the 'routine' or habit, which then leads to a 'reward.' Over time, this feedback loop drives habit formation. In other words, understanding and manipulating this loop is key to breaking negative habits.

18.3. Identifying Negative Habits

The first step towards breaking free from negative habits is recognizing them. To identify a habit, keep an eye out for recurring behavior patterns that have adverse outcomes. As you evaluate your habits, remember to consider both their immediate and long-term effects.

A useful method to identify negative habits is keeping a habit journal. Over several weeks, note down your daily activities, emotional state, and any triggers you notice. As patterns start to reveal themselves, you'll be better equipped to embolden changes.

18.4. Building Awareness

Building awareness about your negative habits is key in the breaking down process. Many harmful habits sneak under our radar due to their automatic nature. To raise awareness, practice mindfulness during your daily routines. Mindfulness keeps your brain in the present moment, interrupting the automated habit cycle. Mindful attention can potentially help you spot the cues that trigger your unwanted habits.

18.5. Replacing Negative Habits

Muster ample diligence because replacing a negative habit might be the hardest part of the process. Begin by selecting an alternative positive behavior. When the cue for the unwanted habit surfaces, consciously engage yourself in the new action instead of the habitual one. Remember, the new habit should deliver a reward that is at least as satisfying as the old one.

18.6. Building Resilience

Breaking habits is a complex process and it's normal to face setbacks. Prepare yourself for the possibility of lapses and relapses. Use these occasions to better understand your cues and motivation. Instead of being hard on yourself, approach failures with a growth mindset, viewing them as learning opportunities.

18.7. Seeking Professional Help

In case the habit you're trying to break is deeply ingrained or is affecting your mental health, seeking professional help is advisable. Therapists, counselors, and other mental health professionals are trained to guide you through the habit-breaking process, offering support and strategies tailored to your specific needs and behavioral patterns.

18.8. Building a Support System

Enlisting the help of friends and family can make the journey to breaking free from negative habits less wearying. Sharing your goals and progress with them can keep you accountable. Moreover, they can offer the much-needed encouragement during tough times. Find your tribe and let them into your world.

18.9. Importance of Self-care

Lastly, while you work towards breaking negative habits, don't forget to take care of yourself. Include regular physical activity, balanced nutrition, and rest in your routine. Practice self-love and celebrate small victories along your path.

In summation, breaking free from negative habits is indeed possible. It might take time, patience, and perseverance, but with an understanding of your habits and a plan in hand, you are equipped to embark on a transformative journey of lasting wellness.

Chapter 19. The Role of Relationships in Mental Wellness

Human beings are inherently social creatures. From the moment of our birth, we are intertwined within a web of social interaction that determines the course of our evolution as individuals. The relationships we form, and the quality of these relationships, have enormous influence on our mental, emotional, and even physical wellbeing.

19.1. The Importance of Relationships

The importance of relationships in our lives can hardly be overstated. From family ties and friendships to romantic connections and social acquaintances, the network of relationships we weave impacts our sense of identity, purpose, and fulfillment. These relationships provide us support, challenge us, instill a sense of belonging, and are a source of personal development and growth. When these relationships are healthy, they can be wellsprings of happiness, stability, and well-being. But when they are not, they can deplete our energy, sour our outlook, and contribute to a decline in mental health.

Because relationships play such a paramount role in our lives, understanding their complex dynamics and our role within them is fundamental. And indeed, science has much to say on the matter. For instance, numerous studies have found that strong social connections can lead to a 50% increased chance of longevity, improve immune response, and lower levels of anxiety and depression. Conversely, low social interaction is linked to outcomes as detrimental as smoking, high blood pressure, and obesity.

19.2. Building Healthy Relationships

Creating and maintaining healthy relationships, in all their forms, is a skill that can be developed with mindful attention and practice. Here are some pivotal elements to keep in mind:

1. **Open Communication**: All relationships are built on the free and respectful exchange of thoughts and feelings. This includes constructive criticism, the expression of needs and desires, and the sharing of thoughts and ideas. Avoid blame and judgement, always focus on understanding and empathy.

2. **Mutual Respect**: Every individual, including you, deserves respect in a relationship. Celebrate each other's uniqueness and value individual differences. Boundaries are an integral part of this respect and should always be acknowledged and upheld.

3. **Reciprocity**: While relationships do not always 50-50, there should be a sense of reciprocity in the mutuality of give and take. Continual imbalances can create resentment and negativity.

4. **Flexibility**: Changes are a part of life and relationships should adapt to evolving circumstances, while maintaining their core values.

5. **Support**: An essential element of a healthy relationship is support. This means both giving and receiving help, encouragement, and understanding during challenging times.

19.3. Overcoming Relationship Challenges

Like everything in life, relationships can go through ups and downs and face challenges. Here's how you can navigate such issues:

1. **Proactive Resolve**: When conflicts arise, address them openly and with a desire to resolve. Sweeping issues under the rug or avoiding them only leads to future resentment.

2. **Cultivate Forgiveness**: Holding onto past hurts hampers a relationship's growth. Learning to forgive is not just beneficial to the relationship but also for your personal mental peace.

3. **Seek Professional Help**: When things get hard, it's okay to seek help. Therapists and counselors are trained to help individuals and couples navigate through relationship challenges and facilitate healing and improvement.

19.4. The Role of Relationships in Mental Wellness

Finally, let's dive deeper into how exactly relationships contribute to mental wellness.

1. **Source of Support**: Relationships provide emotional support during stressful times, lessening the impact of the stress and enhancing resilience.

2. **Uplift Mood**: The sense of connectedness and shared joy in relationships uplifts mood, lowers stress, and contributes to overall happiness levels.

3. **Promote Self-Growth**: Healthy relationships encourage personal growth, self-discovery, and development. They inspire us to become the best version of ourselves.

4. **Cascade of Biochemical Benefits**: Positive interactions in a relationship stimulate the hormones associated with stress-reduction and feelings of love and safety, providing a natural boost to mood and health.

To sum it up, relationships reflect the human need for connection, and strongly influence mental health. While difficult at times, they offer worthwhile rewards in the journey towards mental wellness, making us more resilient and fulfilled individuals. Therefore, cultivating healthy relationships is not just beneficial, it's essential in the path to holistic wellbeing.

Chapter 20. Lifelong Commitment: Sustaining Your Wellness Journey

To embark on a wellness journey is to commit to a lifelong process of growth, optimization, and nurture of the whole self. It's crucial to remember that wellness is not a destination; it's an ever-evolving path that requires constant attention, dedication, and adaptability. The journey can challenge you, but it can also feel invigorating and can create a version of yourself that you never knew existed. We'll discuss the key aspects of making and keeping this commitment: cultivating the right mindset, creating a wellness culture, taking common stumbling blocks into stride, and ensuring steady progress.

20.1. Cultivating the Right Mindset

The first step in this lifelong journey is fostering a sustainable mindset geared towards wellness. Start by identifying your 'Why.' Your 'Why' is the foundation of your willpower, it is what drives you towards your wellness journey. It should be something personal and strong enough to pull you forward even during challenging times.

Your goals will need to be SMART (Specific, Measurable, Achievable, Relevant, and Time-bound). This doesn't mean fixed or rigid. On the contrary, they should evolve as you grow and as your understanding of wellness deepens.

Building resilience is another essential aspect. Life is not without its hardships, but mental resilience can help cushion those blows. Developing resilience starts by recognizing that suffering is a part of life but does not define it. Engage in cognitive restructuring—an exercise where you consciously adjust your thought processes to perceive situations differently. For example, rather than thinking, "I always fail when it gets tough," you might think, "I have the strength to overcome tough situations."

Cultivating gratitude can reinforce your wellness mindset. Practicing mindfulness and gratitude is a great way to appreciating everyday joys. Keep a gratitude journal, reflect on your blessings, and talk about what you're grateful for to start nurturing a grateful heart.

20.2. Creating a Wellness Culture

One person alone cannot create a culture; however, everyone can contribute to it. A wellness culture is a support system—a safe, encouraging, and constructive place that helps you maintain your wellness goals.

Your environment highly influences your behaviors and actions, so choose your surroundings wisely. Surrounding yourself with the right people who are supportive, positive, and health-conscious can greatly influence your commitment towards your wellness journey.

At home, you can promote a wellness culture by incorporating healthy habits into your family's routine. Simple changes like cooking healthy meals together, regular physical activities, and engaging in constructive dialogue about health and wellness can make a significant difference.

Workplaces can also support your wellness culture. Companies today understand the importance of employee wellness and often provide resources such as wellness programs, gym memberships, and access to health-related workshops.

20.3. Taking Stumbling Blocks into Stride

It is important to remember that your path to wellness will not be straight or smooth—it will have unexpected twists and turns. Therefore, be ready to face challenges along the way.

Plateaus, occasional slips, and backslides are common and should not deflate your motivation. If, for instance, you feel stagnant in your journey, consider this as your body's way of preparing for the next phase. It's a good time to reassess your goals, consider alternate methods or simply to rest and rejuvenate.

Failure is one of the biggest stumbling blocks in any journey. When faced with failure, it's easy to question your competence and let self-doubt creep in. However, failures need to be seen as stepping stones, not hurdles. They provide valuable insights into your mistakes, helping you solidify your strategy and bounds you back stronger.

20.4. Ensuring Steady Progress

Progress is a major catalyst for motivation. Whether it is losing the first pound, seeing your mental health improve, or finding joy in physical exercise, progress validates your efforts and reaffirms your commitment.

Keeping track of your journey can play a significant role in maintaining steady progress. Regular check-ins, whether daily, weekly, or monthly, allow you to monitor your progress and adapt your strategies to ensure optimal results.

Developing rituals and routines is another effective way to facilitate steady progress. These set patterns of behavior, when repeated regularly, can automate healthy habits and make it easier to adhere to your wellness regimen.

Finally, don't forget to reward yourself. When you reach a milestone, make sure to take the time to celebrate. Rewards are not just an acknowledgment of progress; theyre vital for motivation. Just ensure that your rewards align with your wellness goals.

Remember, the journey towards wellness is an ongoing one. This guide is here to help you steer your way, provide comfort when you falter, and celebrate with you as you reach milestones. Remember to be kind to yourself during this process; take on the journey one step at a time and remember that lasting changes take time. You are on your own unique path of transformation and growth, and every step forward, no matter how small, is a victory in itself.

www.ingramcontent.com/pod-product-compliance
Lightning Source LLC
Chambersburg PA
CBHW071128260726
48661CB00006B/2729